IMAGES
of America

AROUND
HALLOWELL

The Hallowell riverfront, c. 1890.

IMAGES
of America

AROUND
HALLOWELL

Bob Briggs

ARCADIA
PUBLISHING

Published by Arcadia Publishing
Charleston SC, Chicago IL, Portsmouth NH, San Francisco
CA

Library of Congress Catalog Card Number: 2008938748

For all general information contact Arcadia Publishing at:
Telephone 843-853-2070
Fax 843-853-0044
E-mail sales@arcadiapublishing.com
For customer service and orders:
Toll-Free 1-888-313-2665

Visit us on the Internet at www.arcadiapublishing.com

The Hiram Fuller House, c. 1875.

Contents

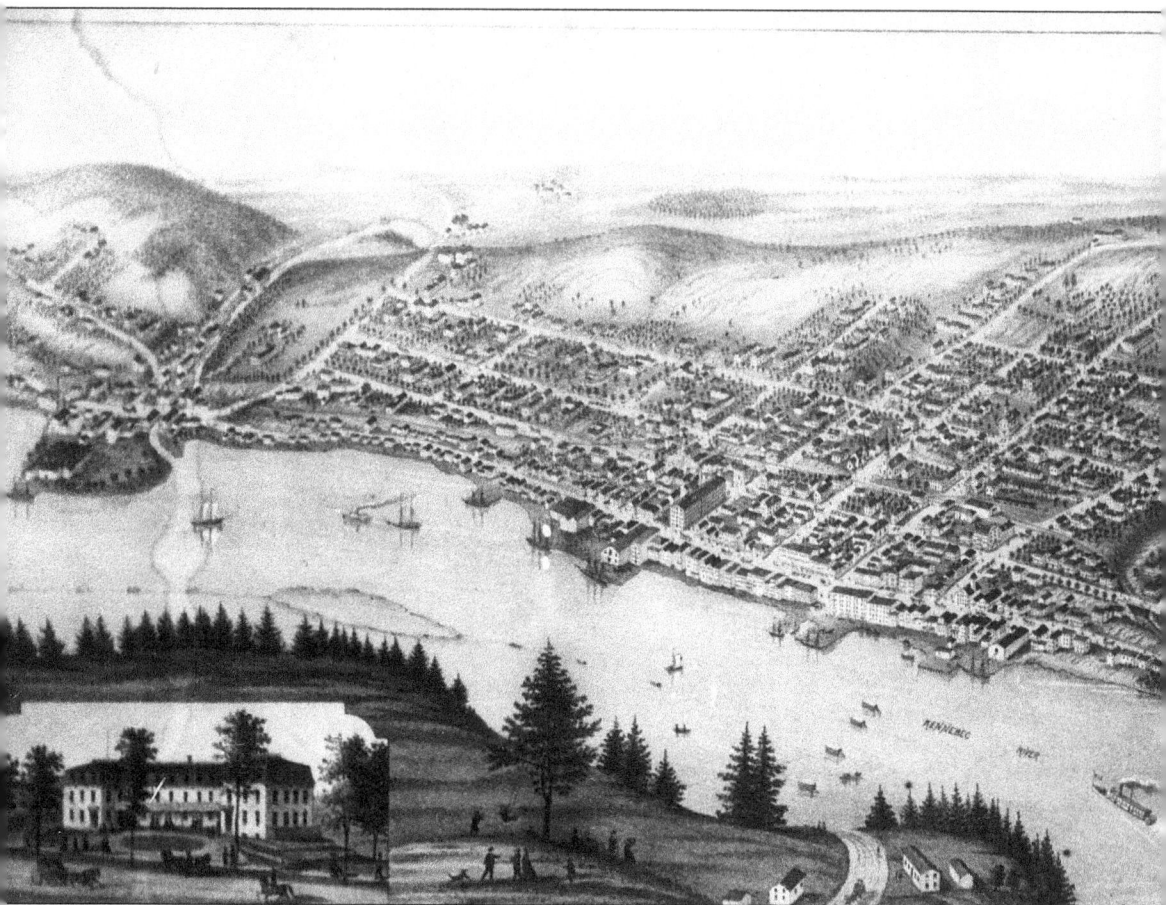

A map of Hallowell, with the Classical and Scientific Institute in the inset. This "bird's eye view of the city" was drafted in 1878, and gives the reader a view of the city as it appeared from across the river in Chelsea, atop Ferry Hill. The map details Hallowell homes and businesses from Shepherds Point (at the far left) to Hinckley's Point (north toward Augusta). Listed in the index are twenty-six prominent landmarks with an alphabetical index for churches.

Introduction

I often wondered as a boy what went through the minds of the early explorers that made their way up the uncharted waters of the Kennebec River in search of suitable land to establish settlements and a trading post. I had read of the handful of men who, in the fall of 1607, boated up from the newly established colony at Popham looking for an opportunity to build a trading post, which they did in 1628 on the present site of Fort Western. Could they have conceived of the tremendous hardships that were yet to come? Probably not. Skirmishes with the Mohawks and Abenaki Indians and the rigors of the long, cold, Maine winter left the lands of the Cushnoc Patent idle for almost a century. And what was their attraction to the wooded, hilly, track of land that would later become known as Hallowell?

I can recall seeing the spectacular view of the Kennebec River Valley as a ten year old, building cabins and looking for buried treasure atop the Ledges, near the crest of Powderhouse Hill. It was easy for me to see what had inspired Deacon Pease Clark and his family to leave their comfortable home in Massachusetts to become the first permanent settlers of Hallowell. It is recorded that Clark and his sons were granted almost all of the 90-square-mile tract that included the present Hallowell, Augusta, and Chelsea.

Was Deacon Clark merely taking advantage of a good deal cut by land proprietor Benjamin Hallowell, or did he foresee that, given its strategic location, Hallowell could one day become a prosperous trade gateway to Boston and other lucrative ports?

Soon to be joined by his family, Clark built a house facing the river on what is now Academy Street, becoming Hallowell's first official residents. Unfortunately, he was not aware that serious trouble was already brewing between the Royalists and Patriots. Soon, the Revolutionary War would pit settler against settler, and settler against proprietor. Inflation, taxation, and conscription cost the newly charted settlement its tranquility and a good portion of its male population.

The first decades of the next century brought separation from Massachusetts and an influx of settlers to the new state of Maine. In a few short years, Hallowell's population would nearly triple. New political alignments across the U.S. and abroad caused shipping and other industries to blossom in Hallowell. Sea captains, farmers, and lumberman began to prosper as never before. Visionary businessmen like George Fuller, Alden Sampson, and Joseph Bodwell brought an unforeseen prosperity to the city in the areas of manufacturing, oilcloth, and granite.

Newspapers and publishing houses flourished, making the city a center of literary achievement. Native sons like John and Jacob Abbott became prolific authors, enjoying an almost national readership. Educational facilities like the Hallowell Academy and the Classical and Scientific Institute drew scholars from across the country and Canada. Hallowell was now on the map, and receiving serious consideration as a possible location for the new state capital.

The Hallowell of my youth represented little of those glorious days. The Kennebec River, once the life blood of a prosperous city, had turned foul and polluted. The stately mansions, once home to the areas elite, were run down, unoccupied, and decaying. The proud city that had once challenged Augusta for the state capital had become its bedroom, and acquired instead a new title: "the antique capital of Maine." Hallowell's eyes were clearly on its past.

My eyes were also toward a time when the streets of Hallowell bustled with excitement and were filled with merchants and shoppers. I would frequently wander back to those days through the images in old photographs displayed in the antique stores, and those that decorated the walls of city hall and the library.

After the final bell would ring at the old junior high, my associates and I would make our pilgrimage downtown, visiting Parents Market, Curtis' Drugstore, Hayes Bakery, and other colorful establishments en route to five minutes of study at the Hubbard Free Library.

Mr. Tibbets, Mr. Boynton, and Etry at the corner drugstore were often eager to discuss things pertaining to that glorious period of Hallowell's past. Others were not so favorable. "Stuff yer pockets and get out of my store" was a popular expression of one store clerk not always appreciative of my frequent questionings.

Now, after so many years, I have felt led to compile, in pictorial form, a history of those special days of Hallowell's past. The story of Hallowell's prosperity should be told to a new generation, before the images and recollections of the era are lost and forgotten.

This book is dedicated in part to the students at the Hall-Dale Primary School, who spend their recess time on the area that was once part of the great oilcloth industry. And to the workers of the local Dairy Queen, who view the parking area that was once center stage for exhibitions held at Muster Field. And to the residents of Joppa, or "Joppy," as they prefer to call it, people who well know the blight of so-called urban renewal.

The book consists of a series of over 220 photographs that span the years 1850–1945. The photographs are taken from collections at the Hubbard Free Library, The State Historic Preservation Commission, and from the private collections of many Hallowell citizens. The captions are often as accurate as the fading recollections of those who lived through those days, and the sometimes conflicting accounts of newspapers and other source materials of the time.

Travel with me now as we turn back to a gilded age when life was more tranquil and less boisterous, when terms such as interdependence and networking were practiced at the community level. Come with me for a nostalgic tour, around Hallowell . . .

One

Around Hallowell

Looking down the Hallowell Chelsea Bridge into Hallowell about 1865. The 1807 edition of the American Encyclopedia predicted that Hallowell would one day become one of the nation's largest cities. Although the city would never fulfill that lofty expectation, by the end of the nineteenth century, there may have been no city in Maine that stood higher than Hallowell.

By the turn of the century, Hallowell had become an interesting, enjoyable, and prosperous place to live. Sea captains, politicians, businessmen, and others of repute built lovely homes, many of which endure to this day. An advanced educational system emerged featuring the Hallowell Academy and the Hallowell Classical and Scientific Institute. Several churches, whose pulpits were filled by some of the ablest preachers of the day, were built to service the spiritual needs of the community. A public library, several newspapers, and a publishing house made Hallowell a center for learning and enlightenment. In addition, a picturesque landscape of ponds, streams, woods, and fields made Hallowell a treasured home for its inhabitants.

Hallowell City Hall shortly before its dedication in 1899. This building remains home to Hallowell's municipal offices and its city manager. Overhead, the stately ballroom and terrace have been used for weddings, inaugurations, and theatrical performances. Since 1900, the building has also been the headquarters for the Hallowell Police Department.

Hallowell City Hall and the post office building at the bottom of Winthrop Street, c. 1903. By 1901, the fire department had vacated the Diplock building, which served a number of tenants including the post office. The post office, repeatedly chased by flood waters on Water Street, held many locations before settling into its present space on the corner of Winthrop and Second Streets.

The Hallowell Fire Department at their new annex on Second Street, about 1910. The city can trace an active fire department all the way back to the Washington administration of the 1790s. The fire department moved to its present location on Second Street either at the end of 1899 or 1900.

The Hallowell Firemen's Association Band, c. 1900. Perhaps due to the risk involved in their profession, the fire department became a close-knit organization. Activities enjoyed together outside the firehouse included the Firemen's Association Band and a baseball team. Challenges were issued to other fire departments to come to Muster Field and see whose pumpers could throw the furthest spray of water.

The Hallowell Library on the corner of Second and Central Streets, c. 1890. To the right is the Johnson Shoe building, a neighbor for the next sixty-five years. A library was first established in Hallowell in 1842 under the name of the Hallowell Social Library. In 1880, the building that remains to the present was erected on the corner of Central and Second Streets. The building represented the cumulative efforts and generosity of many of the city's notable businessmen. Granite for the structure was supplied by J.R. Bodwell and the Hallowell Granite Works. Iron cresting was provided by the Fuller Brothers Iron Foundry and architect plans were drafted by A.C. Currier. An area newspaper reported the library as being "modeled by a Hallowell man, constructed by Hallowell workman of Hallowell material, and paid for by the liberality of Hallowell people." In 1893, General Thomas Hubbard awarded the library a large sum of the money with the request that the privileges of the library be free to all. The name was subsequently changed to the Hubbard Free Library.

Inside the Hubbard Free Library c. 1905. The interior of the library would not change appreciably over the next ninety years. The patrons would. Seated from left to right are Mrs. Earnest Currier, Miss Georgia Wells, Mrs. Ben Tenney, Mrs Susan Currier Sewall, Miss Abby Eveleth, and Mrs. Julia Wells.

The Universalist church as it appeared c. 1900. Beneath the church was a butcher shop. To its right was the church's vestry, which was later turned into the American Legion Hall. The church closed in the late 1930s and became the home of the Rialto Movie Theater, a popular Hallowell attraction in the 1940s and '50s.

The Old South Congregational Church before it was destroyed by fire in 1878. An early record states that Hallowell's settlers first focused their attention on building a church, so that they might make good Christians of their children; they then turned to building a school, so that their children might become good scholars. At the turn of the century, the city was filled with both. The Christian influence in no small way shaped the moral fabric of the community as well as the educational system. From Water Street up, no fewer than nine churches of various denominations served the spiritual needs of the community. On Water Street, Quakers and the Salvation Army held services in rented halls and other areas.

Rebuilding the steeple at the Old South Congregational Church, c. 1884. Originally built in 1796, a fire on December 1, 1878, claimed the church's famous cupola, organ, and the wooden portion of its structure. From 1883 to 1885 the church was rebuilt using Hallowell granite, and a 127-foot steeple was added.

The First Baptist Church, c. 1880. Located on Union Street, this building was the site of the Unitarian church until 1868, when declining interest forced the sale of the building. The new owners, a Baptist group from across town, made several alterations to the church, including a bell that was purchased jointly with the city. The bell was used to call residents both to fire and to worship.

Catholic Ch
Hallowell me.

Looking up at the Sacred Heart Catholic Church, *c.* 1901. To the right is the church rectory. In 1878, land was purchased by a group of Catholic believers weary of the long walk to Augusta or North Whitefield needed to celebrate Mass. This church was finished in November of the same year, and renovated in 1900.

The St. Mathews Episcopal Church, *c.* 1905. Episcopalians in Hallowell first met in the Unitarian church in the late 1850s. In December of 1860, they moved into their own facility opposite what is now the First Baptist Church on Union Street.

The Cox Memorial Methodist Church, *c.* 1912. Methodists first came to Farmingdale, then known as Bowman's Point, around 1800. They moved to Hallowell in 1810, and in 1826 a building was erected on the church's present site. The church was named in honor of Hallowell native Melville B. Cox, who became the first Methodist missionary to Liberia.

The Central Street office of the Hallowell Granite Works, *c.* 1905. Note the carriage wheeling down Central Street, viewing the activities. One of Hallowell's most prosperous industries at the turn of the century was granite. The Hallowell Granite Works was founded by Joseph Bodwell, who would go on to further notoriety as state governor in 1887.

The completed Hallowell Post Office, May 1, 1932. A post office has been in operation in Hallowell since 1794. In 1930, city fathers decided to allocate funds to be used for the construction of a new post office to stand on the corner of Winthrop and Second Streets.

OCT 1, 1931

Workers survey the post office foundation, October 1, 1931. It took contractor Henry E. Plante & Sons nearly nine months to complete the new post office. In the background is the city hall building; to its right is the Depositors Trust Bank building.

The Hallowell House at the corner of Winthrop and Second Streets, c. 1855. One of Hallowell's most significant landmarks is the old Hallowell House. Construction of the building began in 1832 with the hope that it would offer accommodations that would rival those of neighboring Augusta. Hallowell, Augusta, and Portland were all, at this time, vying for the honor of becoming the state capital.

Although it did not succeed in bringing the capital to Hallowell, the Hallowell House attracted famous patrons from all over the country. Theodore Roosevelt and other U.S. presidents stayed here, as well as renowned literary figures like Henry Wordsworth Longfellow and Nathaniel Hawthorne. In recent years, Maine notables L.L. Bean and Senator Margaret Chase Smith were frequent guests at the inn.

The building has changed hands many times over its long history, being mortgaged and foreclosed on several occasions. From 1855 to 1870 it closed its doors all together. The restaurant section has been closed for many years and the building now operates as an apartment complex.

The Hallowell House looking down Second Street, c. 1880. The Hallowell House opened in November of 1834, two years after construction began. Hallowell architect John D. Lord constructed the basement of the building with Hallowell granite and its upper three stories with brick. Fireplaces, high ceilings, and winding staircases were installed to give it a European flavor.

The Worster House and barber shop, c. 1929. In 1915 the building became known as the Worster House and ran many successful years under the proprietorship of Thomas and Pauline Worster. At its peak, the Worster House employed up to eighty persons and was said to consume up to 1 ton of coal per day in the winter. The Worsters closed the building in 1959.

The Powder House on the top of Powder House Hill, c. 1910. The Powder House was built shortly before the War of 1812, perhaps by the Hallowell Light Infantry, or another militia group present at the time. The building fell into serious disrepair before it was renovated in 1948 by a local DAR group.

The old Beeman cannon facing the river on Powder House Hill, c. 1900. Known as the Thunder Jug of Hallowell, it was captured from the British brig *Boxer* in 1813. It came to Hallowell in 1839 by the generosity of Captain John Beeman, and was fired off on the Fourth of July for many years. The cannon remains a fixture on Powder House Hill, in close proximity to the Powder House.

A bridge over a dam on Vaughan Brook, c. 1905. The view is being enjoyed by a local family. Just below is the Sandpaper Mill, whose chimney shows through the trees at left. From left to right on the bridge are Mary J. Stevens, Susie Stevens, Fred Lynn, Lena Lynn, and Mrs. Lynn.

The Cascade Dam at Vaughan's Woods, c. 1900. One of the city's greatest natural resources is the scenic tract of land on the south side known as Vaughan's Woods. Complete with nature trails, hiking paths, and a pond, the woods extend from the Litchfield Road to the back of the Hall-Dale High School. The area has been known as Hobbit Land by at least two generations of high school students.

Canoeing on the Kennebec River, *c*. 1895. One of the best views of Hallowell can be seen from the Kennebec River. The river was a great recreational spot for fishing and swimming until pollution caught up with it in the 1950s and '60s. Arthur Rich and Aaron Norton are the gentleman enjoying the canoe ride. Note the logs to the left. Scalliwags (unmarked logs) were finders keepers to those with a pickpole to get them.

The Crabtree Nursing Home about 1940. This series of buildings located off the Town Farm Road has served the city in a number of capacities over the years. As early as 1870 it was known as the Poor Farm and was used to house the city's indigent and mentally ill. It was later purchased by the Crabtree family and used as a nursing home before ending up as an orphanage in the 1950s. The buildings burned in 1958, and the lot remains vacant.

A trolley headed toward Hallowell at Milikens Crossing, c. 1898. The advent of the trolley made traveling around Hallowell and to points beyond quicker and cheaper. By 1915 over 150 miles of trolley track were in service linking Hallowell with most of central Maine.

Inside the trolley station, c. 1895. This image was taken at one of the two facilities used to house the cars of the Augusta, Hallowell, and Gardiner Railroad in the Hallowell area. One sat at the foot of Loudon Hill in Hallowell and the other was just above what is now Paul Blouin Honda in Augusta.

Two

Water Street

Water Street looking toward Augusta, winter 1870. Like many nineteenth-century New England cities, Hallowell evolved via its access to a significant trade route. The Kennebec River, which brought the first settlers to the area in 1762, also brought trade, industry, and opportunity to its inhabitants over the next 150 years. Merchants became quick to exploit Hallowell's key geographic location as a crossroads for the entire state, where water and land transportation systems met. By the 1850s, Hallowell became known nationally for its exports of ice, oilcloth, wood products, and granite. Linked by schooners and steamers, Hallowell merchants dumped their wares into ports at Boston, New York, and beyond.

As Hallowell grew so did the importance of its main street, aptly named Water Street. While merchants delighted in having export facilities at their back door, they often had to endure the ravages of an unpredictable and unforgiving river.

The backside of Water Street as seen from Ferry Hill, Chelsea, c. 1890. From the river, the city is geographically designated by two points: Shepard's Point (facing south) and Wilder's Point (facing north). The above photograph shows Temple Street to Shepherd's Point with the F.S. Wingate Wharf being prominent. The upper horizon shows farmlands and fields that were left mostly undeveloped until the 1950s.

The Hallowell riverfront looking west toward Augusta, c. 1890. Prominent is the Cotton Mill (left), the steeple of the Universalist church (center), and Hallowell High School. Off the photograph to the right is the Kennebec Wharf and the cove area, and beyond these, Wilder's Point.

A busy day on Water Street, about 1885. This scene is looking down Water Street heading toward the state capital in Augusta. Traffic appears to be headed south toward Gardiner. The absence of the electric railroad line indicates that this photograph was taken sometime before 1890. Horse-drawn carriages were still the main mode of transportation of the day and would continue to be so for the next twenty-five years.

Water Street at a standstill, c. 1880. Note the gas lamp hanging overhead; such lamps came to the city in the 1850s. Bicycles were an important and economical means of traveling around city streets. A.F. Morse and Son was one of many local merchants selling bicycles in the late 1880s.

Interested residents look on as workers lay track for the electric railroad in 1890. In November of 1850, a steam locomotive made its way through Hallowell, forever changing the status of Hallowell as an essential port city. The emergence of the railroad would all but eliminate the need for the schooners and steamers that had made Hallowell an important stop en route to Boston and other major markets.

The advent of the railroad opened up travel and interlinked other towns and communities along the Kennebec River Valley as never before. Following in the steps of the railroad was the electric car, or trolley. In 1890, the Augusta, Hallowell, and Gardiner Railroad was established, linking the the towns with about 7 miles of track. By the end of the 1930s, another innovation would mark the end of the electric railroad: the city bus line.

Awnings decorate store fronts on Water Street, c. 1895. The west side of Water Street boasted no fewer than fifty small business and practices in the 1890s. The range of businesses included dentists, lawyers, grog shops, fish markets, drug stores, grocery stores, barber shops, candy stores, poolrooms, and a roller rink.

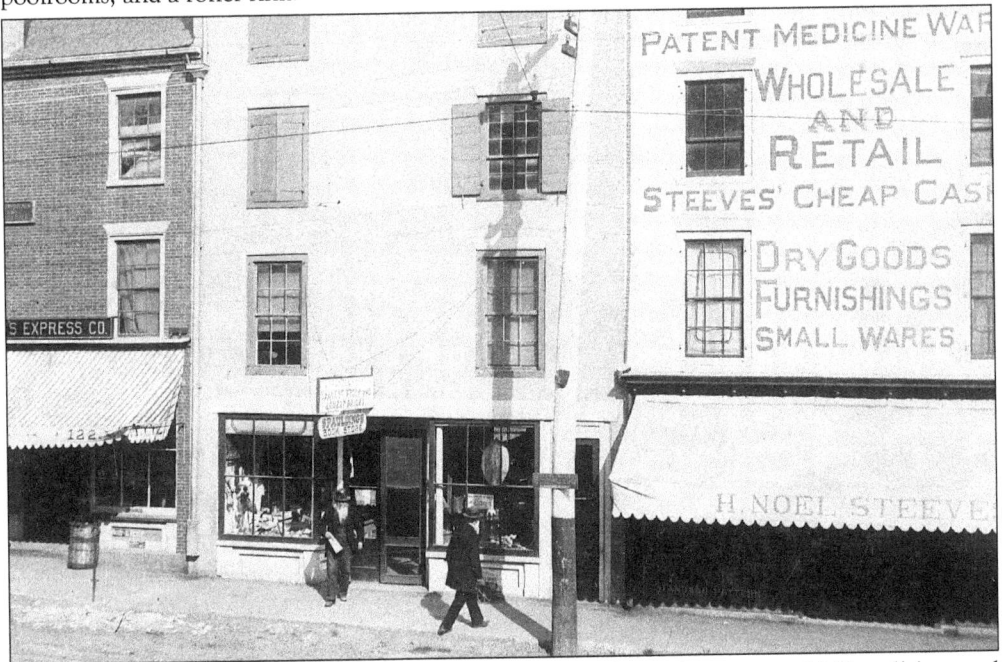

The east side of Water Street, c. 1890. The patent medicine business in Hallowell boomed in the late nineteenth century. Although alcoholic beverages had been banned in the state, a powerful elixir made from opium and Rye Whiskey was distributed widely by the Hallowell Patent Medicine Company, and was made available without a prescription.

The F.S. Wingate building as it appeared in the early 1920s. Family businesses have long been a fixture in the Hallowell business landscape. In 1842 George F. Wingate established a business on Water Street that remains to this day. Four generations of the Wingate family have helped supply necessities to the residents of Hallowell for the past 154 years.

A view of the east side of Water Street, c. 1900. Seen at the near right is the bakery operated by the Hayes family for almost a century. Fires were first kindled in the ovens of the Water Street establishment in 1878.

Customers gather inside a drug store about 1900. This store is believed to be that of Henry P. Clearwater, a Hallowell native who enjoyed great success in the mail-order business of pharmaceutical preparations. His medicines were sold through out the United States, Great Britain, Africa, and other foreign countries. Among his patent medicines were remedies for rheumatism, heart conditions, and stomach ailments.

This photograph precedes Elvis by about forty years. Water Street contained several clothing and tailor shops in the 1890s, offering fashionable imports from home and abroad. This store is most likely Andrews Brothers Custom Tailor & Clothiers, located at the corner of Water and Union Streets.

The Hallowell Post Office, *c.* 1910. The post office made many stops along Water Street before settling into its present home at the corner of Second and Winthrop Streets. Postmaster Morris Fish is the gentleman standing in the doorway. Carrying mail along routes had begun in the winter of 1909, with Arthur Lord (far right) becoming one of the first carriers. Mr. Fish's salary in 1909 was set at $1,900.

A hardware store on Water Street, *c.* 1890. Hardware stores that sold everything from stove pipe to homemade whiskey were commonplace on the street at the turn of the century. Proprietor H.P. Getchell is shown here with Fred Chapman, and to left, City Marshall Al Henderson.

The corner of Water and Union Streets about 1900. To the left is Augustus Morse, no doubt the author of many of these images. George Morse is stepping outside of George Rummel's Barber Shop. An unidentified family looks on from above from a tenement apartment, which were common over many stores.

A Water Street grocery store, c. 1880. Located on the corner of Water and Academy Streets in the 1880s was the AKP Grover Grocery Store. Note the granite hitching posts, undoubtedly cut from renowned Hallowell granite.

An active and prosperous Water Street in 1909. At left, hot dog stands, bakery carts, and other mobile vendors competed with established businesses along the street. At right, Alice Judkins and Lizzie Walker appear to be watching a trolley headed toward Augusta.

A carriage competes with a trolley, c. 1895. The carriage is on its way to the riverfront, perhaps to be ferried across the river to Chelsea. The scene depicts the revolution of transportation that was slowly taking place at the turn of the century, with the electric trolley competing with the horse-drawn carriage. Soon, the automobile would make both obsolete.

Tuck's Corner, as it appeared in 1906. For many years this was the site of Clement Brothers Grocery Store and Fred Clements Cigar and Candy store. The wooden structures gave way to the bulldozer in 1908, and a large brick building was erected by the Hallowell Savings Institution on the site.

Tuck's Corner from another vantage, c. 1885. To the left facing Winthrop Street was the old fire station. To the left on Water Street, a billboard advertises an exhibition that probably took place down the road at the Muster Field Fair Grounds.

The new Hallowell Savings Institution building nearing completion in 1908. Note the absence of windows on the ground floor. The building would contain a theater and ballroom, and house a drug store for many years. It has most recently been used as a restaurant.

The fire engine Tiger outside the fire station on Winthrop Street about 1865. Purchased by the city in 1836, Tiger had a long stint of service, and has recently been restored and put on display at the station. Perhaps its greatest moment occurred on the afternoon of July 3, 1863, when fire broke out in the downtown district while firemen were off on a sailing excursion. Operated by a dozen or so women, the fire was kept at bay, thus saving the city from what could have been its most devastating fire.

A Water Street celebration, June 1896. The 100th anniversary of the founding of the Kennebec Lodge prompted a celebration. The lodge building has long since been torn down, as has the store to the left. In the background is the steeple of the Baptist church.

Perhaps a Labor Day celebration, *c.* 1899. Labor Day celebrations in Hallowell at the turn of the century were no small matter. A newspaper account reports that festivities included floats, parades, orations, and sporting events held at Muster Field. The evening was capped off by a grand ball held at city hall with music furnished by a live orchestra.

Granite being hauled to port, c. 1890. Everyone made way for the granite slab being hauled down Water Street. Weighing as much as 2 or 3 tons, the slab is probably headed down to Clark's Wharf to be loaded on board the *Jeremiah T. Smith* or the *Edward T. Smith*, schooners owned by the Hallowell Granite Company.

The same scenario about 1895. After being cut from the Haines or Longfellow Quarries located near the Manchester line, granite slabs were dragged by horse teams down Winthrop Hill and across Water Street to be stored in sheds or shipped downriver. With the coming of the railroad in the 1850s, granite was also shipped via rail.

A bicycle repairman enjoys a respot, c. 1900. This is possibly the inside of Getchells Hardware Store. Bicycle retailers and repairs were common along Water Street and could be found in hardware or variety stores. The bicycle repair shop was a tradition that stayed on Water Street until the 1960s.

A dirt-coated Water Street about 1875. Pedestrians and carriages line the street on a busy afternoon. To the right is the Gazette Printing Office, which, depending upon the actual date of the photograph, may have been the printing office of the *Gazette Newspaper*.

Water Street looking north, c. 1880. This picture was probably taken from the roof of the cotton mill. The flat roof seen at the bottom corner was added to the mill in 1867 and was probably the only one on the street. To the right is the oilcloth factory on Wilder's Point. An eastern pier from the remnants of the Hallowell Chelsea Bridge can be seen in the river.

Water Street looking south, c. 1880. This photograph shows the Joppa section of Water Street with Shepherd's Point to the upper right. The schooner docked at the pier could have been taking on ice, lumber, or industrial products from the iron foundry located on the point.

Three

School Days

Hallowell Academy before it was remodeled in 1890. One of the first proposals ratified by town fathers after Hallowell's incorporation in 1771 was to raise money for a public school system. Not counting home schools and other private institutions, no less than twenty separate school facilities have served Hallowell's students from that time to the present.

Schools grew up in the population clusters around the city, and it was said there was once a school building on every corner. Efforts toward consolidation came in the 1950s with the advent of the school bus, and a new elementary school was built on the site of the old Sampson Oilcloth Factory in 1953.

Complementing the public school system at the turn of the century was the renowned Hallowell Academy, and the Hallowell Classical and Scientific Academy. Both were post-high school tuition schools that attracted students from across the United States and Canada, and gave Hallowell a place among the academic elite.

The Warren Street School, c. 1895. This one-room schoolhouse was located across the street from the Classical and Scientific Academy. The school was attended by Hallowell children from 1848 to about 1915, when it was converted into a private residence.

Days end at the Loudon Hill School, about 1920. One of Hallowell's oldest primaries, school was conducted at this location from the 1830s to the mid-1950s. The building continues to serve the community and is presently being used by the Masons.

The Page Street School, February 9, 1912. Belle Hopkin's class took time out from a spelling lesson to pose for this photograph. The slate blackboards seen throughout the classroom probably came from Stickney, Page and Company, who had a slate mill located on Vaughan Stream.

The ninth grade class at the Lakeman Grammar School in 1902. Located on the corner of Chestnut and Middle Streets, the school was built in 1882 and served as a primary school for many years. Later it became the English High, or the last grade before high school.

The eighth grade class at the North Mann Grammar School in 1902. Built in 1848, this school was located at the corner of Middle and Union Streets. The building was sold after the completion of the Maria Clark School and converted into a private residence.

The Maria Clark School, September 1906. Named for its benefactor, Maria Clark, the school was an early attempt to consolidate the various grades scattered across the city. The building, renovated in 1947, was later used as a special education school and cable T.V. studio.

Inside the Maria Clark School, spring 1918. Seated is Francis Emery's well-behaved ninth grade class. The school would remain until the 1980s when it was converted into an apartment and condominium complex.

A school-wide assembly at the Hallowell City Hall in 1923. The scene is set on the location now used as a driveway for the Hallowell Police Department. The event was recalled as being a school-wide assembly to dedicate a memorial by Judge Beane (standing beside the flag).

Hallowell High School, c. 1895. In 1887 the school committee decided to start a new city high school, and make it separate from the Classical and Scientific Academy. City fathers chose to renovate the old Hallowell Academy building, which they did in 1890.

Students congregate around the front doors of the new Hallowell High School, c. 1923. Growing enrollments forced the building of a new high school that appeared at the corner of Warren and Central Streets in 1920. In June of 1960, Hallowell united with the neighboring town of Farmingdale to establish a new school district and erect a new high school. Hall-Dale High School was the name of the new facility, which was completed in 1962.

The Hallowell Classical and Scientific Academy, about 1880. The academy was located on the lot at the corner of Central and Warren Streets until its buildings were razed in the early 1900s. It was designed to provide students with a college preparatory education. Insufficient funding forced it to close in 1888.

Students gather outside the Classical Academy, about 1885. The school attracted students from all over the U.S. and Canada and admitted both genders, a novelty at the time. The ladies resided at the ladies hall at the school, and many of the male students boarded in a large rooming house at the corner of Winthrop and Warren Streets. Note the strange invention on the left.

Students in front of the Hallowell Academy, c. 1880. Incorporated in 1795, Hallowell boasted having one of the first academies in the state. From the beginning, the Hallowell Academy was strictly a classical school and students received their secondary education under some of the ablest and best educated men in the state.

The academy was twice destroyed by fire before a brick building was erected in 1841. From 1868 to 1873, the academy and the high school were united, before the Classical and Scientific Academy on Warren Street was opened in 1873. In 1888, the academy building became Hallowell High School and in 1890 it was enlarged and remodeled to accommodate an influx of students. Today it stands as a private residence.

The Hallowell Industrial School for Girls on Winthrop Street, *c.* 1880. The school's first annual report in 1876 described the school as a "home for the friendless, neglected, and vagrant children of the state." The report referred to the young ladies as "inmates." The facility was renamed the State School for Girls in 1915.

The Industrial School for Girls shortly after it opened in 1875. A contemporary newspaper account called the school a "refuge for viciously inclined girls between the ages of seven and fifteen." In the 1960s the complex was known as the Stevens Training Center for Girls. Today the buildings house state agencies and a pre-release center.

The Hallowell High School men's basketball team of 1928. Athletics have long been an important part of education in Hallowell. This photograph was taken on the floor of the gymnasium that legend says was a converted swimming pool. Deafening crowd noise and unyielding brick and concrete walls made for less than ideal playing conditions.

The Hallowell High School women's basketball team of 1927. Note the modest uniforms of the day. The team members are, from left to right: (front row) Olive Cummings, Hermaine Dufresne, Dorothy Dawbin, and coach Dorothy Giddings; (back row) Yvonne Beaudoin, Audrey Johnson, Ruth Johnson, Paulina Clark, and Helen Graves.

A Hallowell High School football team, c. 1922. This team picture was taken on the front steps of the new high school building on Warren Street. Football at Hallowell and later at the Hall-Dale High School was played for almost a century until the sport was dropped after the 1990 season. The school played crosstown rivals like Cony and Gardiner in the early years.

A Hallowell High School baseball team, c. 1927. The team played its home games on the land donated by the Vaughan family off Lincoln Street. The site was the former location of the Sampson Oilcloth Factory and is the present site of the Hall-Dale Primary School. Games were also played downtown at Muster Field.

A men's baseball team, c. 1930. For many Hallowell men, baseball did not end after graduation. From left to right are: (front row) Bill Johnson, Fred Harwood, Max Johnson, Albert Sawyer, Milton Ballard, Mac Masciadri, and Bill Duplessis; (back row) Clarence Turner, Hugh Petee, Stanley Church, unknown, Delmont Luce, unknown, Reginald Trask, Donald Leighton, and Dr. Batchelder.

The Hallowell High School graduating class of 1898.

Four

Industry

Motorists head up Academy Street, c. 1910. According to a published report, Hallowell once had the opportunity to displace Detroit as the spawning ground for the automobile industry. As early as the 1850s, two Hallowell men designed and constructed a steam-powered horseless carriage as a leisurely pursuit. In 1858, George McClench and Judge John Rice displayed their vehicle before a curious and somewhat skeptical crowd as they drove their car from Joppa to the Augusta line. The novelty of the project soon wore off and they scrapped both their idea and the vehicle.

Between 1860 and 1910 industry flourished in Hallowell. By 1890, the town boasted of a shoe factory, two sawmills, two oilcloth factories, two iron foundries, a sandpaper mill, and a nationally acclaimed granite works. A logging industry put Hallowell on the map as a boom-sorting center. In the winter months, great ice houses stretched along the river supplying further jobs and notoriety to Hallowell residents. Supporting these great industries were numerous small business and boutiques that dotted the city streets.

A look up Vaughan Stream, *c.* 1865. Industry grew up in Hallowell along the banks of Vaughan Stream, also known as the Bombahook. As early as the 1790s the Vaughan family had established a flour mill, and John Shepherd a brewery. By the 1880s, a wire company, slate mill, and sandpaper mill were all located along the stream.

The Boston Flint Paper Company, *c.* 1890. The Boston Flint Paper Company was located at the foot of Greenville Street before the railroad tracks. Owner Ben Tenney experimented with many substances for his paper before settling on quartz. Tenney got glue for his paper at the George Seavey Glue Factory, just up the street in Farmingdale.

Workers pose for a photograph outside the sandpaper mill about 1900. From left to right are Bert Grimes, Arthur Rich, Frank Butler, Bert Blair, and Bill Overlock. The operation was considered hazardous to the health of employees, who inhaled fine particles of quartz and other materials used. The mill continued production into the 1920s.

The Kennebec Wire Company, c. 1875. Further upstream from the sandpaper mill was the Kennebec Wire Company, which began operating about 1870. Heavy gauge wire was sent to the plant where it would be reduced to differing sizes all the way down to the finest known at the time. The building was taken over by Ben Tenney in the 1880s and converted into an isinglass factory that made a product useful in brewing beer.

The Elias Milikens' Sons sawmill about 1880. This sawmill was located in the cove to the south of Shepherd's Point. The mill had its origin on a raft that would move up and down the river from job to job. As work increased, a permanent location was sought, and at high water the raft was pulled ashore and a mill built around it.

Believed to be the inside of a Knickerbocker Ice Company shed, c. 1885. Ice was cut from the river in swaths about 1 mile north and 1 mile south of Shepherd's Point. It was either stored in the sheds located at the end of the point or loaded directly onto schooners. Kennebec ice was sent to major port cities like Boston and New York and as far away as Cuba and the West Indies.

An ice house along the Kennebec River, c. 1890. The ice industry came to Hallowell in 1820 almost by accident. Captain John Bradstreet, unable sail his vessel when cold weather hit, decided to tie up in nearby Randolph for the winter. Hoping to claim something from his adversity, Captain Bradstreet stowed away river ice in the hold of the ship, which he later sold at a distant port for a good profit.

A farmer prepares to plow ice, c. 1885. By the 1890s, ice houses dotted the landscape from Hallowell to Richmond, employing over 15,000 men. It was said that farmers found it more profitable to use their plows for harvesting ice than for turning up their fields.

An overview of the many industries that grew up along the Bombahook, *c.* 1885. To the far left is the Boston Flint Paper Company; at dead center is the George Fuller & Sons Iron Foundry; and in the foreground is Millikens Sawmill. To the right and at the end of the point are the Knickerbocker Ice Houses.

A Second Street view of the cotton mill, *c.* 1875. Built in 1844, this building originally stood three stories high with a pitched roof and a tower at the west end. In 1867, another story was added and a flat roof installed.

The paymaster's office adjacent to the cotton mill factory, *c.* 1870. Ownership was apparently celebrating an election victory. The image between the flags appears that to be that of Ulysses S. Grant, which would date this photograph as being in November of either 1868 or 1872.

Inside the cotton mill, *c.* 1870. For its first fifty years, the building housed a cotton mill. At its peak, the mill contained over 15,000 spindles requiring about 200 operators. The mill produced over 68,000 yards of goods per week that included jeans, sheets, prints, and coat linings. The mill was shut down in 1890, and the building changed hands several times in the next sixty years. It was renovated in the 1970s to become housing for the elderly.

The Johnson Brothers Shoe Company, *c.* 1903. Situated on the corner of Central and Second Streets, the Johnson Brothers Shoe Company was for many years a prominent Hallowell industry. Its location along the railroad tracks, just down from the depot, enabled a ready access for export. Johnson Shoes became well known throughout New England and as far away as the West Coast.

Johnson Brothers as seen from the railroad tracks, *c.* 1905. The business was founded in 1887 by twin brothers William and Richardson Johnson. The original building was three-and-one-half stories tall and faced Central Street. Additions over the years expanded the building from the corner of Second Street all the way up to the railroad tracks. The factory closed in 1927 and from 1934 to 1955 it operated as the Kennebec Shoe Company. In 1955 the building was torn down and for many years the lot was used as an ice skating rink.

Employees from the packing room at the Johnson Shoe Factory, c. 1903. From left to right are Julia Sherman, Gertrude Meader, Mary Stevens, Hazel Grimes, Charles Fuller, Ethel Weeks, Ethel Gray, Dana Lynn, Lura Gray, John Smith, and Chick Meader. At its height, the plant employed 350 people.

Eugene Howe and his daughter Mina outside the Howe Candy Kitchen, c. 1895. Employees at break time could visit the Howe Candy Kitchen. The Howe family operated a successful bakery and confectionery shop on Water Street for many years. At its peak, Howe's operated six carts that delivered baked goods to many of the surrounding communities.

The *Eastern Examiner* newspaper and printing company, *c.* 1870. This business was probably located on the corner of Second and Central Streets, before the Johnson Shoe Company operated there. Hallowell has a long history of publishing and its earliest newspaper dates back to 1794, making it the oldest in Kennebec County. Other Hallowell newspapers of notoriety included the *Hallowell Gazette*, the *Hallowell Register*, and the *Maine Cultivator*.

Workers observe another granite creation, *c.* 1905. Located off Central Street were the granite sheds owned and operated by the Hallowell Granite Works. It was said that a piece of Hallowell could be found in every state of the union, an obvious reference to the industry that made Hallowell known as the granite city.

Laborers inside the granite sheds, *c.* 1905. The early 1900s brought the heyday of the granite business to Hallowell. Many Italian and other foreign-born artisans were imported to do elaborate carvings on statues, monuments, and columns. Standing to the left is Joe Varney, with Billy Harkins (center) and George Varney.

Workers applying the finishing touches to the statue of Faith, July 1877. This statute was one portion of the national monument erected at Plymouth Rock in honor of the Pilgrims. Cutting the figure for the Hallowell Granite Company was Joseph Archie, said to be one of the most skillful sculptors in the land at that time.

The Hallowell Granite Works quarry plant at Granite Hill in 1914. Quarried and finished granite is crated, waiting to be shipped, perhaps to finish the state capitol complex in Albany, New York. That one project alone, spanning the years 1867 to 1898, was worth $25 million.

Another view of the quarry plant in 1914. During the last years of the quarry, a spur railroad was installed to move granite slabs. Horse teams were still needed to drag slabs down to rail carts off Winthrop Street or the wharves along the Kennebec River.

Haines Quarry, about 1860. Granite was first quarried in Hallowell about 1815 at Haines Quarry, located on the outskirts of the city near the Manchester line. The cornice stones for Quincy Market in Boston were taken from this quarry between the years 1815 and 1827.

Hallowell granite boxed and ready for shipment about 1900. The Maine Central Railroad accommodated Hallowell's granite industry by supplying extra large cars that were used to ship columns and statutes to distant locations.

Workers take a break at the Hallowell Granite Works sheds off Winthrop Street, c. 1905. By the turn of the century the granite industry employed over five hundred men in various capacities. Quarrymen, carvers, blacksmiths, team drivers, and schooner crews were all needed to deliver a finished granite product to customers nationwide.

Workers construct the dam for Casscade Pond about 1870. Hallowell granite also found favor in its native city, and was used in many architectural projects of the day. The Hallowell City Hall, the Hallowell House, the Hubbard Free Library, and many of the city's fine homes had foundations laid in Hallowell granite. The state capital in Augusta was comprised almost entirely of Hallowell granite.

Quarrymen survey mountains of granite in 1871. By 1880, the Hallowell Granite Company owned the rights to the Haines Quarry and the Longfellow Quarry, owned originally by Governor John Hubbard. A third quarry was located close by giving the area its rightful designation as Granite Hill. Quarrymen worked an average of fifty-six hours per week, their wages ranging from $1.65 to $3 per day.

Workers move granite slabs with a derrick, c. 1880. Blasting powder was used to free slabs as early as 1829. Before that, pieces of granite were quarried by using hammers and wedges. By 1870, derricks were used to move massive granite slabs. By the 1930s, the quarries on Granite Hill had reached a depth of almost 60 feet.

The Hallowell Granite Works city plant as it looked in 1914. At right is the railroad terminus that provided for easy shipping access. Above the rail car is the roof line of the Hallowell House. Houses that lined Winthrop Street appear in the background.

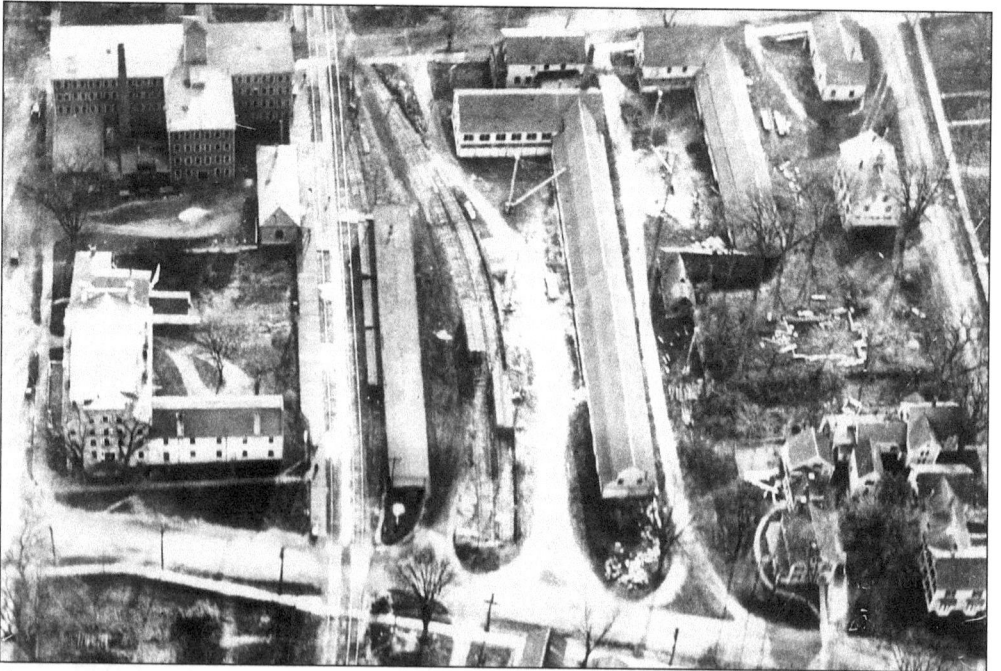

An aerial view of the city plant about 1925. The building on the left is the Hallowell House, now known as the Worcester House. In front of the Worcester House is the Johnson Shoe Factory. To the far right are the granite sheds of the Hallowell Granite Works. Between the shoe factory and the hotel is the railroad depot.

A busy day at the city plant, *c.* 1875. By the 1920s, competition and new technologies had taken their toll on Hallowell's granite industry. Busy scenes like this had become a thing of the past. By the end of the 1930s, springs and rains filled the Granite Hill quarries, which were now stocked with fish. Lewis P. Gipson, the last supervisor for the Hallowell Granite Works, became known as the custodian of a ghost industry.

Monuments for sale, *c.* 1890. This was the retail portion of the Hallowell Granite Works. Note the sheds in the background.

The Kennebec Monumental Works in 1924. The founders of this longtime Hallowell business were Sittinio Masciadri (left) and Tony Perrazzi (far right). The business was located in the present parking lot of the Sandollar Restaurant.

The E.E. Taintor Company, c. 1910. The chief competitor of the Hallowell Granite Works at the turn of the century was the E.E. Taintor Company. The plant was located on Wilder's Point beneath the railroad tracks, approximately the same spot as the former Wilder Oilcloth Factory.

Fido's Filling Station as it appeared about 1930. This building, located at the Joppa end of Water Street, lives on as part of the Sandollar Restaurant. Pictured are three generations of Masciadri businessman: Alfredo, Americo, and Sittinio.

Jimmy Hayes' Socony Station at the corner of Water and Union Streets, c. 1931. The emergence of the automobile brought a new industry to the streets of Hallowell. In 1933, the Mobil Oil company opened a plant on Wilder's Point, and service stations began to spring up all over town.

Steve's Super Service about 1936. This early service station was located on the west side of Water Street. Gas pumps appear to be on what is now the sidewalk. Standing on the left is Perley Stevens; to the right is Happy Christie.

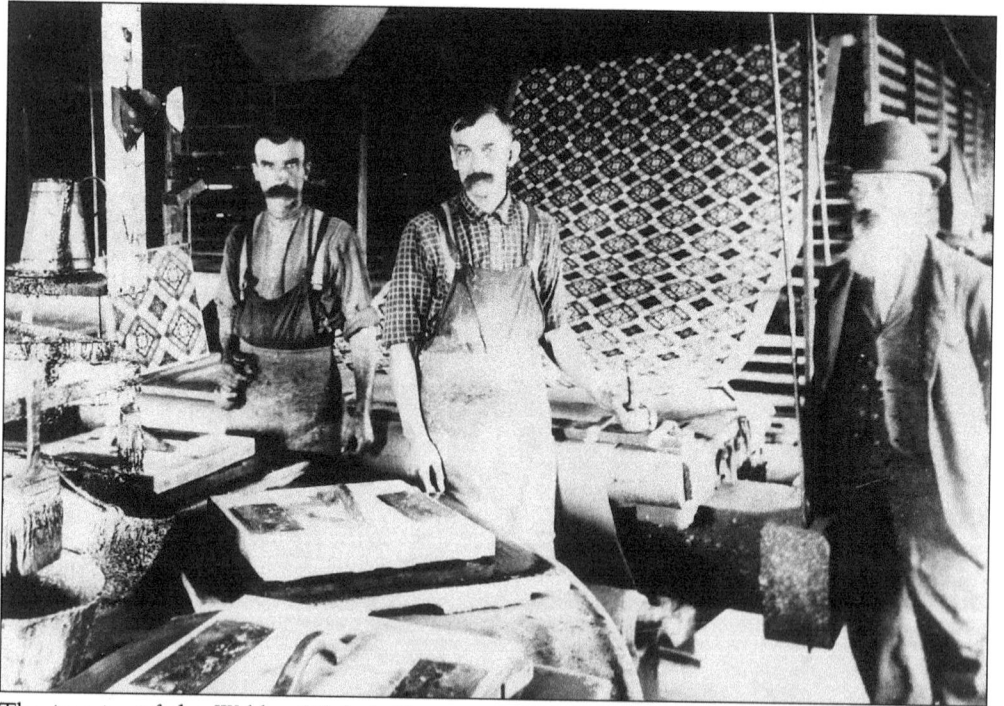

The interior of the Wilder Oilcloth Factory, c. 1895. In the picture, from left to right, are Charles Bailey, Frank Greeley, and James Jones. Hallowell operated two oilcloth factories, one off Lincoln Street and the other on Hinckley's Point. The latter was bought out by Dr. Amos Wilder in 1872 and ran continuously until it succumbed to fire on January 13, 1900.

72

Five

Floods

Flood waters invade Hallowell, April 30, 1923. Hallowell inhabitants have long endured a unique relationship with the Kennebec River. From the river the city gained access to lucrative markets—but from the Kennebec also came the annual threat of flood and its often devastating consequences.

A large snowfall, followed by heavy rains in February and March, nearly always spelled disaster for Water Street merchants and residents. In late March of 1826, the city recorded its first significant flood. This was to be followed by major floods in 1870 and 1896. The twentieth century brought some of the most devastating flooding to the area, when an angry Kennebec rose to unprecedented heights in 1936, and again in 1987. Floods and other catastrophic occurrences have time and again showed the resiliency of Hallowell people, who have always rebuilt and continued on with their lives and livelihoods.

The Hallowell Chelsea Bridge, *c.* 1869. Not even ten years old, the Hallowell Chelsea Bridge became one of the more notable casualties of a rising, raging river. On October 3, 1869, rains began to fall and continued for the next three days, causing the river to rise 22 feet. The two western piers of the bridge came down as a result of the freshet.

The Hallowell Chelsea Bridge, February 1870. The flood of February 20, 1870, claimed the remainder of the bridge. Freezing flood waters resulted in extremely large ice chunks which felled the wooden portion of the bridge, carrying it downriver atop the ice.

Townspeople survey bridge damage, c. April 1870. The bridge was not a complete loss, as redeemable wooden portions of it were used to frame a nearby house. Remnants of the stone and concrete piers can be seen at right. Joseph R. Bodwell, a Hallowell resident and onetime state governor, offered a large sum of money toward the rebuilding of the bridge, but the proposal fell on deaf ears. Beginning in 1871, a ferry enabled residents to travel back and forth from Hallowell to Chelsea via boat and barge. The ferry operated for almost ninety years before closing in 1960.

Remnants of the Hallowell Chelsea Bridge, *c.* 1875. This view is from the Chelsea side looking west toward the Eastern Steamship Company Wharf. Docked at the wharf is the steamer *Clarion*. Of the original seven piers, only three were left standing after the freshet.

Flood waters and destroyed buildings, February 1870. On February 20, 1870, the Kennebec River rose 6 feet in half an hour before cresting at a height 25 feet above its normal level. Broken ice claimed several buildings, including the granite sheds behind Clark's Wharf and some private dwellings.

Glaciers invade the Joppa section of Water Street, March 1870. This scene includes Bodwell's stone sheds and wharf, and other dwellings on the east side of the street. Houses looking on from Second Street sustained no serious damage.

Water Street near the corner of Central Street, March 1870. Large, glacier-like deposits were left behind by the receding river. Patient merchants could only wait for nature to take its course before the street would once again be free for commerce.

The corner of Union and Water Streets, March 1870. Merchants and townspeople gather to assess damage done by the flood. High waters remained for nearly a week and caused the evacuation of all street-level businesses. Among the businesses hardest hit was the *Gazette* printing office, located at right.

Looking south toward Gardiner, March 1870. A lone figure on horseback observes the flood waters that brought business to a standstill for all Water Street merchants. The Joppa area still appears to be flooded, as do the Wingate buildings on the left.

The Hallowell Post Office inundated with water, March 2, 1896. March came in like a lion in Hallowell in 1896. It produced the third catastrophic flood of the century and, to date, the most destructive. Flood waters reached a level some 2 feet higher than the 1870 flood, as recorded on the granite corner of the post office building. Newspaper accounts said that when boats were brought in to navigate city streets at noon on March 2, the city looked like a small Venice.

By March 3, Shepherd's Point, located off the end of Water Street, had become an island. Further downriver the Gardiner Randolph Bridge was swept away and carried toward Richmond by the surging waters.

The Joppa section of Water Street, March 3, 1896. Most suspectible to damage by the raging flood waters were the wood-framed houses that lined the Joppa section of Water Street. Some of the dwellings were moved off their foundations and relocated across the street. Others became houseboats sent floating down the river.

Boaters explore lower Water Street, March 2, 1896. To the left is the engine house where the electric trolley cars were stored, and the plant that produced their electricity. The sturdy brick building has endured the wrath of four major floods. Above the engine house is a portion of the McClench Brothers Machine Shop and Foundry.

Flood waters at crest, March 2, 1896. This view is looking down Central Street in behind Water Street. Now lost from sight is the Kennebec Wharf. Newspaper accounts list a few businesses that were not able to recover from the flood damage. The average business loss was estimated anywhere between $50 to $200.

Looking down toward Joppa at the corner of Academy Street, c. March 6, 1896. Merchants and families sort through their belongings at the edge of Water Street. At right the cotton mill, not in operation at the time, sustained little damage.

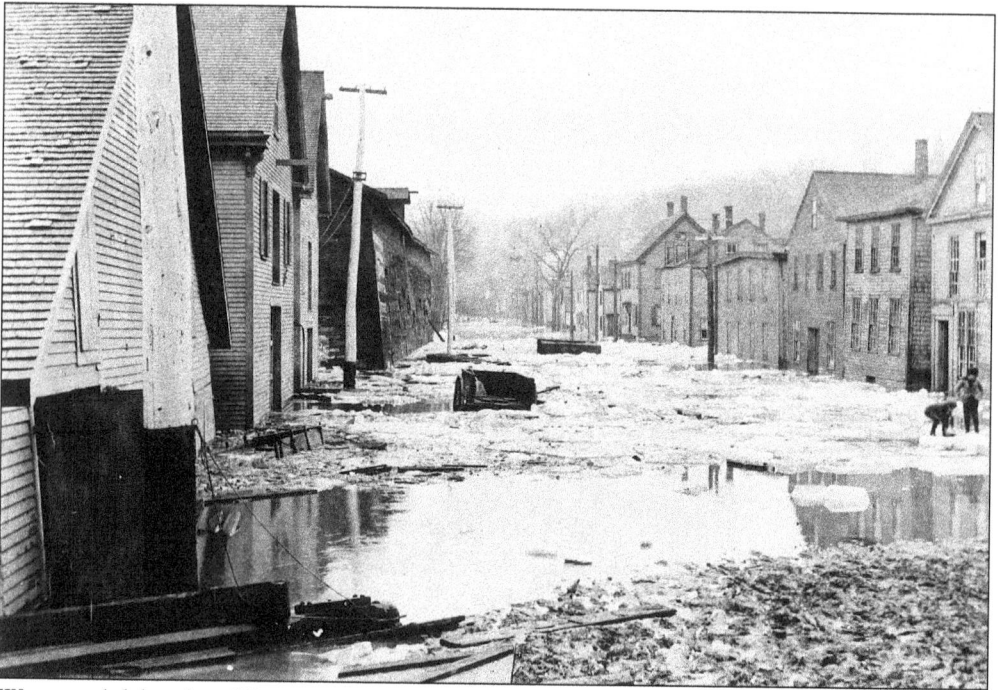

Water and debris line Water Street, March 1896. Although flood waters had receded, pockets of ice and water remained along the street. The children at right explore a small pond while merchants prayed for clear weather.

Business proceeds as usual on Water Street, March 1896. As the waters began to recede, the need for staples like coal brought merchants back to work. An unknown man has stopped his wagon on the coal scale in front of the F.S. Wingate building.

Water Street looking south, *c.* March 9, 1896. Despite persistent rainy weather, activity returned to Water Street. The wet conditions prohibited the use of the electric trolley; despite the muddy road conditions, however, horse-drawn buggies continued undaunted.

Water Street looking north, March 1936. A flooding Kennebec River struck again on March 12, 1936. The flood was unleashed by a combination of heavy snows and an early thaw followed by heavy rains. Flood waters rose to a level 3.5 feet above that of the flood of 1896.

Fido's Filling Station, Friday, March 13, 1936. Fido's had more at the pump than gasoline, with waters reaching even higher levels in the next two days. Considerable damage was sustained by local merchants but even more by Water Street residents. Newspaper accounts suggest that more than fifty families were forced to evacuate their homes.

Looking toward Augusta, March 13, 1936. The business at right is the Kennebec Monumental Works. At the far left is the cotton mill building, now operating as the Kennebec Shoe Company.

Water Street, *c.* March 16, 1936. Motorists plow down Water Street with a still swollen river at right. The small building at right appears to have been upended by the rising waters.

Looking north up Water Street, March 13, 1936. Some residents are boating, some wading, some watching, but all are concerned over the rising waters. The flood would prove to be the most devastating of the century until eclipsed by the flood of April 1987.

Water Street, April 30, 1923. Besides four major floods, the city has endured other occasions when the Kennebec has surpassed its banks. In late April 1923, heavy rains resulted in flood conditions. This scene is looking toward Gardiner with the F.S. Wingate coal building on the left.

Looking up Central Street, April 30, 1923. Water non-withstanding, motorists drive their Model-Ts down Water Street. The building on the right heading up Central Street is Anderson's Clothing Store. The building on the left is Rummell's Barber Shop, followed by Achorn's Tannery.

Workers survey windstorm damage, January 1895. Nature has posed other obstacles that Water Street residents have had to endure. On December 31, 1895, a violent windstorm caused considerable damage to many buildings and businesses. At right an unidentified man restrings telegraph wire. To the left, repairs continue at the AKP Grovers Grocery Store.

Men freeing a horse from rubble, January 1895. Reported to be one of the worst gales ever to blow up the Kennebec River, fierce winds took a portion of the cotton mill's roof. Roof timbers became projectiles inflicting great damage to surrounding buildings. The building being inspected for damage is probably the George Palmer Wood Yard or one of the cotton mill's storehouses.

Concerned bystanders watch the central fire station burn on November 17, 1932. Firemen did not have far to travel to deal with this blaze. Fire has been a twin scourge with water for most of the city's history. It has claimed the life of many Hallowell businesses, the Wilder Oilcloth Factory being the most notable. The Hallowell Academy burned on two occasions, as did the Boston Flint Company building.

Freight cars pay an unwelcome visit to the Hubbard Free Library, November 10, 1937. Three cars from a southbound freight train derailed and smashed through the large gothic window on the building's west side. The window, some rare books, and various museum pieces were lost in the accident.

Six

Street Scenes

Harry Clement drives his rig down Greenville Street about 1900. The streets of Hallowell were bustling with activity and excitement around the turn of the century. Merchants peddled their wares and milkmen delivered dairy and other farm products to the doorstep. Beginning in 1909, postal carriers began making house calls with the daily mail and newspaper. Horses could be seen watering at troughs set at the foot of Vaughan Street and the corner of Winthrop and Water Streets.

Schoolchildren were a frequent sight on Hallowell streets, and other scholars could be seen congregating outside the Hallowell Academy and the Classical and Scientific Institute. Grand houses built by sea captains, businessmen, and politicians graced the streets in tranquil days when the sound of a whinnying horse and rumbling carriage were the only noisy distractions.

Overlooking the Kennebec River, c. 1880. This view is from Powderhouse Hill, probably taken from the Hubbard Barns on the west side of High Street. Prominent are the Classical Institute (left) and the spire of the Universalist church (center). The expanse of the river is seen from Hallowell to Farmingdale.

Looking up Academy Street about 1920. Just before the bend in the road that turns up High Street is the Shepherd Homestead, built in 1910 by Clarence Shepherd and his grandfather, Albert Lord. Shepherd's two sons, Robert and Cedric, built many of the houses on Mayflower Road, Orchard Lane, and other areas above High Street.

90

A motorist's view from the Vaughan Bridge, c. 1903. Seen below is the Joppa section of Hallowell. Note the crib work in the river used to hold back logs scattered on drives. In recent years, the use of the Vaughan Bridge by motorists was discontinued. It eventually succumbed to the wrecking ball, as did most of the tenement houses in Joppa.

The Sawyer family, perhaps on their way to church, c. 1905. Pictured outside their residence on Loudon Hill are, from left to right, Barbara, Hope, Hazel, and Warren Sawyer. The tent was a welcome relief on hot summer nights.

The railroad crossing at Second Street, about 1880. Other than the cupola atop the cotton mill and the steeple above the Universalist church, this scene looks much the same today. Shaded by the oak tree in the background is the Old South Congregational Church.

A locomotive speeds past Greenville Street, c. 1890. At the foot of Greenville Street, the steam locomotive could wave to the electric trolley on its way up Loudon Hill. At left is the Boston Flint Company building.

A horse and driver head across Middle Street, c. 1903. Merchants delivering goods were a common scene around the streets of Hallowell at the turn of the century. Note the wooden walks and sidewalks that made Hallowell's rainy season easier for pedestrians to endure.

A winter walk down Winthrop Street, c. 1890. Gentlemen walk past Hiram Fullers house (left) on their way downtown. The booth at the bottom of the hill was probably used to tend the gate at the railroad crossing just above Second Street.

Looking down Central Street to the riverfront, c. 1885. The *Della Collins* lies docked at the Kennebec Wharf. To the left is the old Beeman Block, long since torn down. The block contained a livery stable, and extended up as far as Second Street. The gas lamp hanging overhead may have been installed as early as the 1850s.

Looking across Middle Street, winter 1900. Riding in the pony-drawn sleigh are Ralph and Walter Moore. The house on the corner is that of Justin Smith, then treasurer of the Hallowell Savings Bank.

A muddy Lincoln Street, spring 1895. Spring thaws and rains brought fresh challenges to Hallowell motorists and carriage drivers. The granite hitching post at left and the telephone pole at right show a city in transition. The building at the far right on the corner is the Captain Merry House.

Looking up Winthrop Street about 1898. The lot on the upper right probably indicates that construction was underway for the new city hall building that was completed in 1899. A carriage can be seen at the intersection of Second and Winthrop, perhaps carrying a dignitary from the capital to lunch at the Hallowell House.

A view of a well-kept Second Street, c. 1875. Since before 1870, a public works department run by the street commissioner maintained the roads in Hallowell. The Hallowell City Report of 1871 listed total expenditures of department to be $4,731.59 for the year. It included an inventory of nine scrapers, two plows, one wheelbarrel, one steel rake, one snowplow, and 6 feet of drain pipe.

A friendly visit, about 1880. The Reverend and Mrs. Parker Jagnes meet with Mrs. Robinson and family outside their residence on the corner of Union and Second Streets. White picket fences were prominent around town during this period.

A look up Second Street, about 1870. The Hallowell House stands prominent at the far left. The house on the corner sits on the present location of the Hubbard Free Library. On the left before the Hallowell House is Palmer's Blacksmith Shop, and across the street is Simon Johnson's Livery Stable.

A snow-covered Union Street, c. 1870. To the right are Niles Livery Stable and Carriage House, which extended all the way to the corner. Up the street on the right is the Baptist church. The spire of the Cox Methodist Church can be seen in the background.

The Vaughan Bridge stretches over Cascade Pond, c. 1903. This stone arch bridge was built by William and Benjamin Vaughan in honor of their father, distinguished Hallowell resident William Manning Vaughan.

Carriage tracks line Middle Street, c. 1895. Although the electric trolley had been in operation on Water Street since 1890, horse-drawn buggies continued to be the most popular mode of transportation on the city's dirt-coated side streets.

Middle Street sidewalks, fall 1901. Note the telephone poles standing at the street corners. By the late 1880s, telephone lines began to spring up along the city streets. In the area's first telephone directory, published in 1881, Hallowell had six listings.

Fire engines head down Second Street, winter 1905. Nothing generated more excitement around the streets of Hallowell than the fire department rushing to a fire.

Granite being pulled down Winthrop Street, c. 1890. Horses were harnessed to the front and back of the massive granite slabs, which were dragged down Winthrop Street to awaiting railroad cars or schooners. Newspaper accounts report several bloody accidents occurring in the early 1900s.

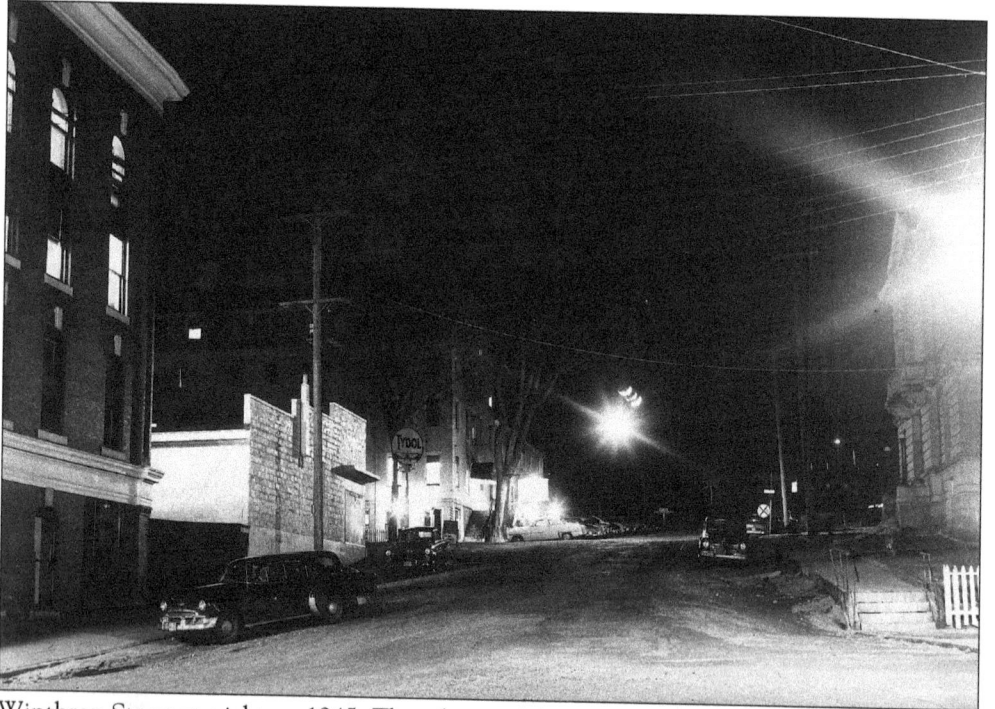

Winthrop Street at night, c. 1945. The advent of the mercury vapor street lamp transformed city streets at night in the 1940s. At right is the city hall building. At left is the Depositors Trust building and a Tydol gas station. On the corner is the Worcester House and Mickey's Barber Shop.

Seven

River Life

The shore of the Kennebec River as viewed from "the British side," or Chelsea, c. 1901. The Kennebec River has played a vital role in the evolution and growth of the Hallowell area ever since Deacon Pease Clark and his family landed on its shores in the fall of 1762. For Hallowell's first 150 years, the Kennebec was the city's lifeline for trade, commerce, and recreation. The river opened up such industries as fishing, logging, and ice cutting. The shipping and shipbuilding industries flourished in Hallowell in the nineteenth century, and the river provided a ready access for Hallowell exports such as granite, shoes, oilcloth, and wood products.

Today the river stands in sharp contrast to its usefulness in Hallowell's heyday. It holds little commercial value and is known chiefly for its recreational resources. Such is a far cry for a city once wholly dependent upon the river for its economic sustenance.

Passengers board the *Islander, c.* 1910. Owned and operated by the Augusta, Gardiner and Boothbay Steamboat Company, the *Islander* was reported to be one of the fastest steamboats on the river. The steamer made daily trips to Boothbay Harbor and other stops up river.

The steamer *Sagadahoc* heads up the Kennebec , *c.* 1890. Originally built in 1866, this steamer was first known as the *Star of the East.* Owned and operated by the Kennebec Steamboat Company, it was built to make the run between Hallowell and Boston. Rebuilt in 1889, it became known as the *Sagadahoc.*

A small steamer makes its way down the Kennebec, c. 1900. Steamers began to make their appearance on the river in the 1820s. Many of the early vessels carried sails as an auxiliary power. By 1850, a profitable steam line had formed that ran from Hallowell to Boston.

A steamer rests at Kennebec Wharf, c. 1899. The vessel is either the *Clarion* or the *Della Collins*. The *Della Collins* was one of the most popular of the shuttle steamers that transported passengers to connect with Boston-bound steamers at Bath, Richmond, and Gardiner. The boat was dismantled in 1906, after a successful twenty-five-year run.

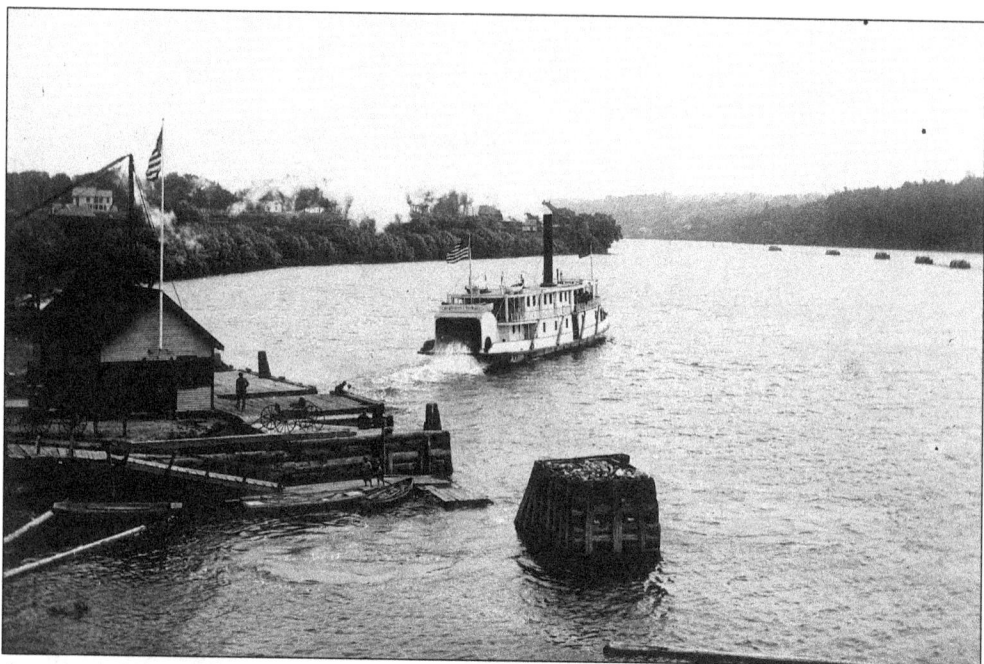

A steamer leaving the Eastern Steamship Company Wharf, c. 1885. The wharf was located at the bottom of Winthrop Street, just up from Wilder's Point. Sitting on the dock are two carriages, probably awaiting transport across the river to Chelsea.

The schooner *Jeremiah T. Smith* at the Hallowell Granite Company Wharf, c. 1885. The *Jeremiah T. Smith* was one of two schooners owned by the Hallowell Granite Company that docked at the company's wharf, which was located below Temple Street. The insert is of the schooner's captain, Leslie Lyons of New Haven, Connecticut.

104

Fording the Kennebec River by ferry in 1917. When the Hallowell Chelsea Bridge washed out in the early spring of 1870, it left an obvious void in access across the river for the residents of Hallowell and Chelsea. Tourists seeking the famous spring waters and resort area at Togus were also pressed to find a new route across the river.

In 1874, a ferry service was established by the City of Hallowell and Kennebec County. Ferry keepers received a wage from Chelsea and Hallowell and a small fare from each passenger. Ferry service at this location continued until the death of longtime attendant Frank Hansen in 1960.

Schooners rest at the F.S. Wingate Wharf, c. 1855. Two and three-masted schooners coexisted with steamers on the Kennebec River for many years. Schooners were used primarily as cargo vessels, transporting granite, ice, and lumber. They were replaced by tugs and barges in the early 1900s.

A small sailing vessel enjoying a tranquil river, c. 1890. Hallowell residents have long enjoyed recreational pursuits along the river, save for a brief period when industrial wastes and sewerage made the river unpalatable. Fishing, swimming, and boating have recently made a comeback as the river has enjoyed a recreational resurgence.

An aerial view of the Hallowell riverfront, c. 1920. Granite was still being shipped from Hallowell in the 1920s and the industry became increasingly dependent upon barges and tugs for its transport. In the center of the picture, at the edge of the water, is a granite derrick ready to load a fresh shipment of granite on the barge.

The view also provides a panoramic view of a riverfront showing signs of decline, as the railroad and trucking industry were making the river less vital. The Old South Congregational Church (center) and the cotton mill building stand prominent. At right, the F.S. Wingate building and wharves can be seen.

Crews rafting logs near "The Gap," c. 1901. The logging industry in Hallowell enjoyed a successful run for almost a century. Log-driving companies would collect their logs at Moosehead Lake and send them downriver to the many sorting booms along the way. The largest sorting boom for downriver mills was boasted to be in Hallowell.

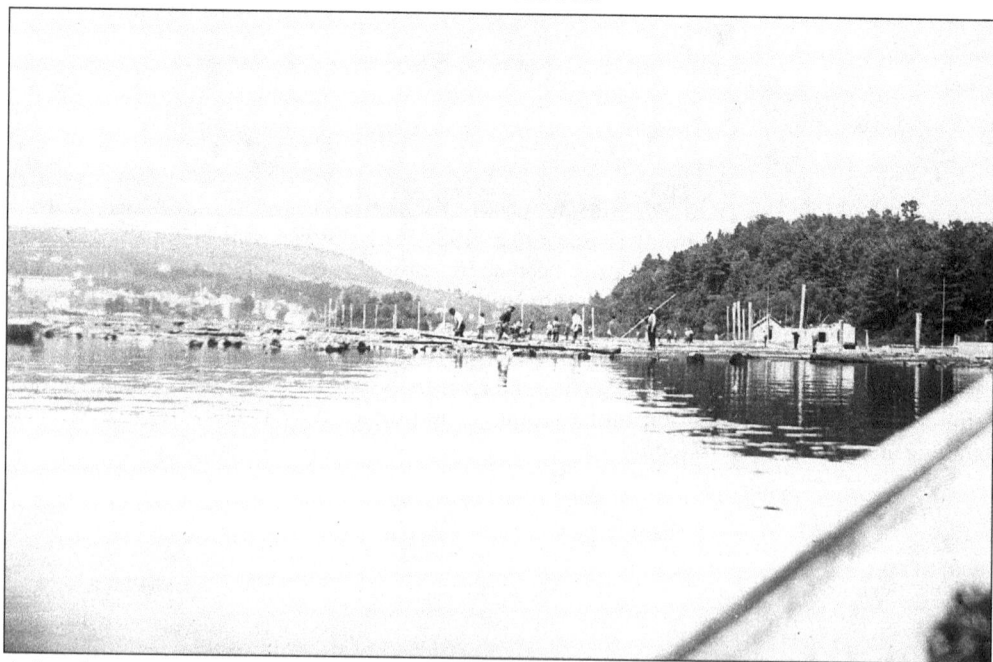

A log-driving crew on the Chelsea side of the Kennebec, c. 1895. Log drivers would float timbers downriver to the sorting booms where they would be picked, sorted, and tied into rafts. Rafts would then be floated and picked up by their owners. At its height, the sorting boom in Hallowell employed between three and four hundred men.

A boom crew awaits another day's work, c. 1901. Workers lived in floating shanties that provided them lodging and shelter from the elements. The shanties were sometimes built two-and-one-half stories high, complete with mess accommodations. At night they were anchored on the Chelsea side of the river.

The tugboat *Farnsworth* headed up river, c. 1903. Tugs and barges slowly began to replace schooner activity on the river in the early 1900s. The newcomers proved much more economical, and provided greater versatility. They also took less manpower to operate and required less maintenance.

A quiet day on the river, c. 1900. Enjoying the day, and perhaps doing some fishing, are George Stevens and Fred Lynn. Fishing on the river was a popular pastime, with eels, sea bass, sturgeon, and some game fish being plentiful. In the background is the F.S. Wingate Wharf.

Winter on the river, c. 1901. Winter in no way brought a cessation to activates along the Kennebec. Ice fishing shacks dotted the river for recreation and profit. Sliding, sleighing, and other recreational pursuits were also enjoyed. Ice harvesting was nearing its heyday as a large and profitable industry when this photograph was taken.

Eight

Faces and Places

The home of Hallowell librarian Annie Page, c. 1915. A distinctive characteristic of nineteenth-century Hallowell, perhaps more so than any other small city in New England, was that it attracted to itself many prominent and influential citizens. The list included renowned artists like Alger V. Currier and Joseph Archie, authors such as John and Jacob Abbott, leading entrepreneurs like Ben Tenney and George Fuller, and a tradition of gentlemen farmers like William Vaughan.

Hallowell also boasted of several state legislators that distinguished themselves in the political arena, and two residents, Joseph R. Bodwell and Dr. John Hubbard, that held the distinction of being elected state governor. Along with those that achieved fame were the common people that added color and uniqueness to a diverse city.

The Hallowell High School women's basketball team, 1924. Seated in the front to the far right is Grace Blake Maxwell. Mrs. Maxwell holds the distinction of being Hallowell's first, and to date, only, female mayor.

A piano recital, c. 1910. Seated at left is Belle Hopkins, a teacher at the Page Street School for many years. As was mandatory for teachers of the day, she received her education at a normal school, a post-high school finishing school.

Judge Henry Knox Baker, c. 1880. A Hallowell resident since the age of fourteen, Judge Baker had a distinguished career as the editor of the *Hallowell Gazette*, one of Hallowell's longest running newspapers. Knox also served as probate judge for Kennebec County, and was the founder and treasurer of the Hallowell Savings Institution. He was productive into his late years, writing a memoir of Hallowell at the age of ninety-five.

Mrs. Henry Baker, c. 1880. The former Sarah Lord, Mrs. Baker was a lifelong Hallowell resident who married Judge Baker in 1855. The Bakers had one daughter, Martha, who penned three novels and numerous poems.

Hallowell clergyman Americus Fuller, c. 1885. Hallowell distinguished itself with clergymen of notoriety, many of whom became prolific authors and sought after speakers. Reverend Fuller was a longtime pastor at the Old South Congregational Church.

Getting ready for a delivery, c. 1903. A time-honored tradition in Hallowell that stood until the 1960s was the daily delivery of milk and other farm products. Zeri Parker, seated along with his wife, ran a milk route for many years, starting deliveries from their home on the Litchfield Road.

A Hallowell gentleman stands on Water Street, *c.* 1902. A fixture on Hallowell streets for many years, Billy Ellis Hostler is shown here probably looking toward the steamship wharf at river's edge. Across the street, Smiths Livery Stable had moved into the Diplock building after the departure of the fire department in 1900.

Ready for another day is "Petticoat Jack," *c.* 1905. This lady was often seen walking about the city streets wearing a long petticoat.

115

Young men of Hallowell gather for a photograph along Union Street, c. 1902. These gentlemen are standing at the side of Nick Connor's Drugstore at the corner of Union and Water Streets. The building was the original site of the city's first tavern. Ironically, Arthur Boynton, who operated a grocery store at this location for many years, refused to sell beer or alcoholic beverages. From left to right are John Smith, Herbert Shea, Albert Tregembo, Arthur Fish, Ken Fuller, Ralph Carey, unknown, Arthur Douglas, Jim Leighton, Vic Carey, Lester Sinclair, Alton Blaisdell, and Guy Pickard, with Milton and Carl Aldrich in front.

The Chester Stevens family, outside their Greenville Street residence in 1904. From left to right are Chester C. Stevens, Frank H. Stevens, Mary Stevens, and Susie Stevens.

The Hallowell Boys Brigade stand outside headquarters, c. 1905. From left to right are First Lieutenant James Marston, Captain Percy Bradbury, and Second Lieutenant Skidmore. The Boys Brigade was a predecessor of the Boys Scouts and other fraternal organizations for boys.

Dr. Hubbard's office, *c.* 1890. One of Hallowell's most outstanding citizens of the nineteenth century was Dr. John Hubbard. Educated at Hallowell Academy, and a graduate of the University of Pennsylvania Medical School, Hubbard established his medical practice in Hallowell in 1830. His successful practice brought patients from near and far and his consultation was sought by the most reputable physicians in New England. Hubbard's office was for years located on the same property as his residence on Winthrop Street. The office has recently been restored and preserved as a museum. In 1988 it was moved to Second Street, next to the Row House.

John Hubbard Jr., *c.* 1860. Hubbard's accomplishments were not limited to the medical profession. He served as preceptor at the Hallowell Academy and taught school in Virginia before entering medical school. Dr. Hubbard served in the state senate from 1850 to 1852 and later served as governor of Maine. During his term as governor, he signed into effect the first prohibitory law which gained national recognition as "the Maine Law."

The Hubbard Homestead on Winthrop Street, *c.* 1890. This was the residence for many years of Dr. Hubbard and his wife Sarah. The homestead remains much the same today on the outside. The one-and-one-half story house had several attached buildings, one of them being Dr. Hubbard's office.

The Row House on Gage Block. This building was originally built in 1846 by Isaac Gage, son-in-law of John Seawall, one of Hallowell's earliest settlers. The five-apartment tenement was a dwelling for immigrant Italian stone carvers who were imported to Hallowell to work in the granite industry.

Alger V. Currier at home , c. 1890. A Hallowell artist of great renown, Currier was educated in Hallowell schools before studying art at the School of Fine Arts in Boston. He was the son of A.C. Currier, the architect and head draftsman of the Hallowell Granite Works. A.C. Currier also designed the Hallowell Library and other buildings in the city.

The stone house on Winthrop Street, c. 1945. The Hayes family, proprietors of a bakery on Water Street for almost a century, have owned the "granite house" on Winthrop Street since 1901. The house is uniquely constructed of blocks of Hallowell granite, some of which are a foot thick, 3 feet long, and a foot high.

The Artemus Leonard House, winter 1920. This edifice was built on part of the original land grant awarded to the Clark family in 1762. The estate was once owned by Richardson Johnson, co-founder of the Johnson Shoe Company that ran successfully in Hallowell for many years.

121

The Governor Joseph R. Bodwell residence, c. 1885. Bodwell became the second Hallowell man to be elected to the office of governor, although his term in office was extremely short-lived. Bodwell was elected and began his term in office in 1887, and died on December 15 of the same year. A two-term mayor of Hallowell and an entrepreneur, Bodwell can be credited with much of the success achieved by the granite industry in Hallowell. In 1866, he moved to Hallowell from Vinalhaven and resurrected a sagging industry. Bodwell formed the Hallowell Granite Works, and also had interests in lumber, ice, agriculture, and the railroad. A man of high character and integrity, his counsel was sought and esteemed by many.

Governor Joseph R. Bodwell, c. 1887.
Though not a career-minded politician,
Bodwell left his mark on the political
landscape in Maine. He served two terms
in the Maine Legislature before reluctantly
consenting to have his name presented as a
candidate for governor of the state.

The Vaughan Homestead, c. 1925. Built
in 1794 for Hallowell patriarch Benjamin
Vaughan, this homestead has a spectacular
view of the Kennebec River, and to the
west, a protected forest complete with
streams and waterfalls. The city owes much
of its prosperity and culture to the Vaughan
family, who were among Hallowell's first
and most influential settlers.

John Stevens Abbott, *c.* 1860. One of Hallowell's greatest literary minds, Abbott attended Hallowell Academy and Bowdoin College, where he graduated with Henry Wordsworth Longfellow and Nathaniel Hawthorne. A prolific writer, he penned more than fifty books and had a ministerial career that spanned forty years.

Hallowell author Jacob Abbott, *c.* 1860. An author of more than 180 books, Abbott's Rollo book series for boys is still read and is on the shelves of many libraries. His greatest notoriety may be in the founding of Abbott's Institute, and later the Abbott Collegiate Institute, a pioneer work for women's colleges in this country.

The Niles Homestead on the corner of Second and Union Streets, c. 1905. This dwelling is thought to be that of Alden Niles, or it may have been one of the many retirement homes that sprang up throughout the city at this time. Just below, on the opposite side of the street, was the Niles Livery Stable.

A croquet game at the Wells residence, c. 1910. Located on Middle Street, the house was originally built in 1820 by Benjamin Wales. It was eventually sold to Captain Charles Wells, a sea captain of great renown, known for his extensive travels abroad.

Waiting for the horse and carriage, c. 1900. This is the Middle Street residence of Dr. William Chase, who shared a dental practice in Hallowell with his son George. The house was for many years the home of Francis and Doris Harwood.

The Densmore House, c. 1906. This dwelling was located off the south end of the Hallowell House, and for many years was the residence of Dr. Howard Milliken, a longtime Hallowell physician. The railroad depot can be seen in the background.

126

Children congregate outside the family farmhouse, c. 1885. From High Street to the western city limits, the Hallowell landscape was dotted with family farms that supplied fresh produce, meats, and dairy products to area merchants and residents.

The Forrest View Farm on the Outlet Road, c. 1927. This is the Gregoire family, who purchased the farm in 1925. It was used to harvest fruit trees and raise cattle. In the 1980s, the building was converted into a bed and breakfast and is presently known as the Maple Hill Farm Bed and Breakfast.

Acknowledgments

I am grateful for the opportunity to acknowledge the efforts and kind intentions of the many people that helped make this book a reality.

Thanks to my aunt, Ruth C. Briggs, for many years the librarian at the Lithgow Public Library, who inspired and encouraged me to undertake this project.

This book would not have been possible without the efforts of Jack Boynton and others who have been diligent in preserving early photographs of Hallowell. Their collection is presently on display at the Hubbard Free Library. My thanks to Nancy McGinnis and other staff at the Hubbard Free who have graciously borne with my perusal of the many resources available at the library. Easy references to old newspapers and other primary source materials made researching the book that much easier and enjoyable.

Many thanks to Earle Shuttleworth and the Maine Historic Preservation Commission for the use of their photographs. Special thanks to Earle, who has traveled this path before in his own book on Gardiner.

A special thanks to Miss Abby Garofalo, who took time out from her busy schedule of school work and other activities to help in the research and layout of the book. And also to Sam Webber, a true authority on the history of Hallowell.

I am greatly indebted to the generosity of those who added their private collections to this work, Arthur Moore and Fred Worster in particular.

I also acknowledge my indebtedness to those who labored to preserve the history of Hallowell in volumes much more informative and complete than this work.

Thanks to Tim and Elizabeth Nevins for their help in the final layout of the pages.

My final thanks is to Jesus of Nazareth who continues to "Show Himself alive through many infallible proofs" (Acts 1:6).

www.ingramcontent.com/pod-product-compliance
Lightning Source LLC
Chambersburg PA
CBHW050922150426

42812CB00051B/1952